Ruth

IN THE SHADOW OF HIS WINGS

REACHING HER

REACHINGHER.COM

Copyright © 2017 Amy Bufkin & Hannah Snyder

All rights reserved.

ISBN-13: 978-1545514535

ISBN-10: 1545514534

contents

How Nice of You to Join Us 5

How This Works 7

Week 1 - Setting the Stage...................... 9

Week 2 – Chapter 1: Sojourning 19

Week 3 – Chapter 2: Circumstances........... 31

Week 4 – Chapter 3: Risky Redemption 43

Week 5 – Chapter 4: Grand Finale 55

Week 6 – A Look at Redemption 67

How nice of you to join us!

To the depth of our beings, we believe the Bible is buried treasure. But unfortunately, not many people consider studying their Bible a worthwhile investment. We hope the reason you are reading this introduction right now is because you want to see for yourself what kind of treasure this Book holds. Honestly, we are so excited to have you here. Part of our goal in this study is to push you to think and wrestle with Scripture on your own. We aren't going to tell you what to think or believe, but we are going to give you the tools to start digging.

How this works

Grab a Bible (we will be using the ESV) and a good journal. These two things, along with this study, are everything you need to begin **Ruth: In the Shadow of His Wings**. As you press on, we will be standing on the sideline cheering for you and ready to offer a hand if you want one. You'll notice that we have set out a week's worth of study. **Feel free to self-pace the study to fit your life.** Whether that looks like one sitting spent at a coffee shop or seven breakfast table quiet times is up to you. Remember, a deeper relationship with Christ is the prize; so don't worry about when, where, or how much you get done. **Start wherever you can, and grow from there.**

While you grow, we can support you in several ways. Links within the study will lead you to a Resource Page that will help explain the resources used. A weekly blog about **Ruth: In the Shadow of His Wings** will communicate what we are learning, and if you need encouragement, then we have a social media community and a Pep Talk waiting for you. There will also be Reaching Further portions to pursue if you'd like to go a bit deeper into the study. Finally, when you get to the bottom of each week's lesson you will see a section for Discipling Her. **This is designed to use when you come** together in community and can be an effective tool for leaders, groups, or communal discussions.

Please join our online community by tagging **@ReachingHer** in your group pictures and personal posts and adding **#reachingherlovesruth.**

You can take it from here! Know that we love you and will be praying for you.

week 1
SETTING THE STAGE

May you be rewarded for your work by the Lord under whose wings you have come to take refuge.

RUTH 2:12

Ruth: In the Shadow of His Wings

"Once Upon a Time..." is how fairy tales, adventures, and all really good stories start. It draws us in and gets us excited about what is to come. Fortunately for us, Ruth is one of those good stories. But it is more than just a story. God preserved the book of Ruth in the Bible for us to listen to, relate to, and learn from. In this story we meet four main characters. **Naomi** - an older woman who hasn't always made the right choices and has tasted the bitterness of sin. **Ruth the Moabitess** - a bold and humble young woman who is "all in." **Boaz** - a man of excellence in a world that has chosen to go awry. And finally, the **"closer relative"** who is not even named. **So, let's dive in together and see what we can learn from a story that took place a long time ago.**

In order to fully appreciate this truthful tale, we're going to have to do a bit of work to understand the historic culture in which this story took place 3,000 years ago. **Understanding the circumstances that shaped the lives of our characters will help us understand the story itself.**

Let's start by reviewing what was going on in history up to the time of Ruth by looking at the seven books of the Bible that take place before Ruth. Don't worry! We are simply going to do a quick survey of these books: GENESIS, EXODUS, LEVITICUS, NUMBERS, DEUTERONOMY, JOSHUA, and JUDGES. Don't spend too much time here -- this is just a survey.

» *Grab a journal* and write down the name of each book of the Bible listed above. Now using our <u>Questioning Resource</u> let's start flipping through each book and notice the stories you see. Turn your observations into a list under each book's name.

» *Reaching Further: Once we've used the Bible to gather an overview of what these books are about, feel free to use some extra-biblical sources to find more information about each book. Commentaries and internet searches are helpful. Remember to use discretion in your search.*

» Finally, **summarize what you learned about each of these books of the Bible** leading up to the story of Ruth. What do we learn about God and His people?

Day 2 & 3

Now that we've done a broad overview, let's move in a bit closer and learn some specifics about **the culture of Israel** that surrounds this story.

- » God makes a conditional agreement with Israel when he leads his people out of Egypt and towards the promised land. Read Exodus 23:20-33 and **explain the agreement between God and His people in your journal**. Also look at Joshua 23:1-13. What is Joshua reminding Israel? What is Israel to do?

- » Using our <u>Truths and/or Applications Resource</u> is there anything that we can draw to our life from what we've learned about how Israel is supposed to walk with God?

This is a true statement in our lives as well as Israel's: We know what we should do, but we don't always do it. We just saw what Israel was charged to do; **let's find out what God's people did once they were in the promised land.**

- » Read Judges 1. While Israel starts strong, how do they finish?

- » Next read Judges 2-3:8. Because Israel has not

driven out the sinful nations, what will happen (look specifically at 2:1-5)?

» In Judges 2:11-3:8 Israel takes another step farther from God. Make a list of of what Israel chooses to do. Make a list of what God does. What do we learn?

» To sum up how Israel is choosing to live, read Judges 17:6 and 21:24. Write in your own words what we have learned about the culture of Israel at this time. How does our culture relate to Israel's?

» Finally, let's find out when the book of Ruth took place. Look at Ruth 1:1. We can also do a discretionary internet search if we want more historical context about this time.

» Now, **let's apply this to ourselves by considering the following questions:** Do we do the same things as Israel? Is there sin that needs to be driven completely out of our lives? What happens if we choose not to drive out our sin? Prayerfully consider the answers to this question and ask God to show you how to be obedient to the truth.

Day 4 & 5

We've looked at Israel and now we are going to look at the other big piece of our historical context - the nation of Moab. **Let's find out what it means to be a Moabite as compared to an Israelite.** We will be using our Cross Reference Resource, and there are quite a few of them, so hang in there! This will help us understand the whole story of Ruth, because **Ruth is from Moab.**

- » Let's begin by reading Genesis 11:27 and 19:30-38. How would you identify Moab and their relationship with Israel?

- » Now let's move on to Joshua 24:9, Revelation 2:14, Deuteronomy 23:3-4, and Nehemiah 13:1-3. **How does Moab treat their "cousin" Israel?**

- » *Reaching Further: Take a break and enjoy an adventurous story that happened between Israel and Moab close to the time of Ruth. Judges 3:15-30. What do you learn about the relationship between these two countries?*

- » Next let's find out **what it was like to be the people of Moab?** (You are doing great!) We'll look at Genesis 13:1-12 (remember Lot is Moab's dad, and

Ruth: In the Shadow of His Wings

Moab inherited part of his land), Jeremiah 48:11, 42, and Isaiah 16:6. What do we learn?

» *Reaching Further: Visuals help us grasp concepts. Start by doing an internet search for a map of the "King's Highway." What is it? Where did it go? What benefit would Moab receive by being on the King's Highway?*

» **Can we identify with the Moabites?** Are there any major overarching Truths and Applications for us from understanding this people group?

» Even though we sometimes choose to behave like Moabites, even though justice would cry for us to be cast out of the assembly of God, God doesn't wish that for us! In fact, God always makes provision for us to come to Him. That's what Jesus is about. **Even in the Old Testament, see how God makes provisions for Moabites to come to Him** and to His temple by looking at Isaiah 56:3-7.

» Let's write a prayer to God. Let's praise Him by telling Him what we have learned and ask for His help and guidance for any applications we need to make.

Congratulations! We just built a time machine and took ourselves back to approximately 1100 BC. We've earned an understanding of where God stands, where Israel stands, and where Moab stands. It's interesting how much we are like Israel and Moab. **We know what is right, but will we choose to do it, to walk in it, to live it out?**

The stage is set and now we're ready for the story to begin. Next week get ready to meet two of our core players, Naomi and Ruth...

Truths & Applications

Discipling Her

Suggestions for Leaders & Disciple-Makers

> » Share what you learned about each book of the Bible leading up to Ruth. Did you discover anything you had not seen before?

> » What did you learn about Israel's walk with God? Could you apply anything to your own life?

> » Considering what you learned in Judges, how important should we treat the sin in our lives? What are some ways you can drive out sin and help others drive out sin?

> » Even though Moab chose to make poor decisions, God's mercy triumphed over their mistakes. In the same way, Jesus offers us the same mercy. What are some ways you have seen this mercy in your life?

week 2

CHAPTER 1: SOJOURNING

Every story has a beginning. A starting place. An embarkation. It sets a tone for where the story is going, and it sheds light on what is to come. Lesson 1 gave us a foundation of context for Ruth, and now it's time to start building the narrative.

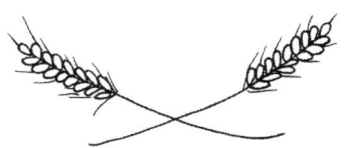

Day 1

So, this is it. This is the moment we get to dive into this rich story!

- » Let's prayerfully read through Ruth chapter 1 a few times, taking note of all the characters that are mentioned.

- » There are four main characters we are going to identify and mark throughout the whole book. Two are introduced this week - Naomi and Ruth. While we read, let's use our Key Word Resource to mark every reference to these two women - you may want to use different colors or symbols for each character.

- » Let's use our Summarizing Resource to get a grasp on each verse of chapter 1.

- » *Reaching Further: It may be helpful to make a little family tree of Naomi's family for reference later.*

Tomorrow we are going to take some time and break down this chapter in more relatable portions.

Reread Ruth 1:1-5

- » Let's use our <u>Word Study Resource</u> for "sojourn" (also seen as "live for a while" in some translations). It is Strong's #1481. Compare that to a modern dictionary definition and take note of what you learn.

- » Are there references to how long Naomi and her family "sojourned" in Moab?

- » Now, let's go back and review the historical context we learned last week about the nation of Israel and the time of the Judges (specifically Judges 21:25). What kind of times where they living in?

- » Let's think about Naomi and her family's actions. Were they good or bad? What would you have done in similar circumstances?

- » Consider this quote:
  - ○ "Sin will take you farther than you wanted to stray, keep you longer than you wanted to stay, and cost you more than you wanted to pay." Wayne Barber

- In light of what we have read and considering our own lives, does this quote ring true? Why?

» It is said that we are either moving towards God or away from Him. There is no middle ground. We want to take some time to meditate on where we find ourselves today. Which way are you moving?

Reread Ruth 1:6

» Why did Naomi finally decide to go back home?

» Let's read the following cross references: Exodus 4:31, Jeremiah 29:10, Zephaniah 2:7, Psalm 132:15, Matthew 6:11.
- What do we learn about God's character and what He promises His people?

» Now let's look at Romans 2:4 and answer the question: How does God's kindness affect us? What do we learn about God's character? Is that how you view God?

» Take some time and take note of any major Truths and Applications God is showing us by using our Truths and Applications Resources.

Day 3

Reread Ruth 1:8-13

- » This is an intimate and sensitive scene to begin our story. How would we summarize Naomi's actions and words?

- » Let's step into her shoes for a moment. What do you think of her response? Would you think and act similarly?

- » Naomi's choice of words is very interesting. What blessing does Naomi give her daughters-in-law in verse 8?

    - o The word for "kindly" (Strong's #2617) will be an important word to know for this whole study. Let's use our Word Study Resource and write down what we learn. What does the usage of this terminology say about Naomi and her view of the Lord?

    - o Now let's focus on a phrase in verse 13: **"the hand of the Lord has gone out against me."** (Other translations - "the Lord's hand has turned against me") Let's use our Cross

Reference Resource to find other places in the Bible where this phrase is used. What do we learn? How does that help us understand Naomi's mindset?

- » Naomi seems a little divided in her view of God. Why?

- » How do you view God? Does your view of God change when you sin and experience consequences as compared to when things are "good"?

- » Are there additional Truths and Applications we can add to our list from this section?

Day 4

Reread Ruth 1:14-15

- » Orpah makes a choice that Naomi validates - what is it?

- » Let's see if we can find anything about the gods to whom Orpah was returning. Do a simple internet search of "gods of Moab." How would we describe the character of their gods?

- » What do you think about Naomi choosing to go home to the one true God while Orpah went home to these gods?

- » How can we apply that to our own lives? Do we always point others to the one true God?

Reread Ruth 1:16-18

- » **Time for Ruth to take her first stand.** How would we summarize her plea to Naomi?

- » Step into her shoes. What do you think about her response? What does it say about her character? Would you do the same?

Day 5

Reread Ruth 1:19-22

» Let's describe the scene as Naomi and her Moabite daughter-in-law walk back into Bethlehem.

» Focus on verse 20. **Naomi gives herself a new name.** What does Naomi's new name mean compared to her old one? Why did she change her name? A discretionary internet search should easily provide that information if it isn't included in our Bibles.

» *Reaching Further: Jewish tradition focuses on the importance of names. Do an internet search to gain some context on Hebrew names. Then go back and look up the meaning of the names of everyone in chapter 1.*

» What is Naomi's perspective in verse 21? Looking up the definition of "brought calamity" ("brought misfortune," "afflicted," Strong's #7489) may be helpful. What does this phrase say about Naomi's view of God and her current circumstances?

> Naomi is "in a state" for sure, but is this the right perspective? Is having a correct perspective necessary for us? Why?

What a beginning! **This story is full to overflowing with action and emotion. It is easy to get caught up in it all.** But we must remember Ruth is ultimately a story full of wisdom about our God.

Each week we want to meditate on exactly what He is revealing about Himself and our lives. One way we will do that is by ending our lesson with writing out a brief summation of each of the main characters. This week that would be Naomi and Ruth. Then we will end by going back through and listing (or adding to our list) our major takeaways - Truths about God and Applications for our lives.

And if you think this beginning is good, wait until chapter 2!

Truths & Applications

Discipling Her

Suggestions for Leaders & Disciple-Makers

» After reading Ruth 1, what are your first impressions of the main characters?

» What is the culture of the nation of Israel during this time? Do you think that affects the decision-making process in Naomi's family?

» Who causes famines? Why?

» Why does Naomi decide to return home and what are the responses of her daughters-in-law?

» What is going on in the heart of Naomi as she returns to Bethlehem? How do you think she feels about God? Have you ever felt the same way?

CHAPTER 2: CIRCUMSTANCES

Circumstances come and go causing alternating waves of difficulty and ease. **A lot of the time we can't control our circumstances, but we can control our responses to them.** So what do we do when we are in the midst something hard? What do we do in the midst of favorable times? In chapter 2 of Ruth we see our main characters in very different situations. Let's see what we can learn from each of them.

Day 1

» First, prayerfully read chapter 2. **Get caught up in the story; it's a great story.** After enjoying it, let's go back and use our <u>Key Word Resource</u> to continue to mark references to the main characters. Don't forget to mark Boaz -- he makes his debut in verse 1.

» By this point we've read chapter 2 several times and are beginning to have a grasp on what's happening. Sum up in your own words the circumstances that Ruth finds herself in and then do the same for Boaz and Naomi. Finally, **pause and take a moment to list the circumstances that you currently find yourself.** We'll come back to this later.

Next we're going to study chapter 2 all the way through three times. **We will study it through the eyes of Ruth, spend a short moment with Naomi, and then we will change to the perspective of Boaz.** This way we will reap three full harvests of truth.

- » Let's look at where we marked Ruth through chapter 2, using our Listing Resource to note what Ruth says and does. How could we describe Ruth? What do we learn about her emotions and about her actions?

    - ○ Here are two cross-references that give us more insight into what Ruth is doing in chapter 2. Look up Leviticus 19:9-10 and Deuteronomy 24:19-22. What do we learn about God? Ruth?

    - ○ Let's look at verse 12 again. What does Boaz state that Ruth has done? Let's use our <u>Word Study Resource </u>to look at "**REFUGE**," Strongs #2620. What insight into Ruth's choices does this give us? Does this shed any more light on Ruth 1:16?

- Next, let's use our <u>Cross References Resource</u> to learn more about God as our refuge. Perhaps start at Psalm 36:7. What do we learn?

- *Reaching Further: Ruth does the hard labor of a foreign widowed pauper for how long? Look at verses 21-23. Do an internet search to see how long Ruth gleans in the fields. Are there any applications on perseverance and hard work that we can apply?*

- Make a list of Truths and/or Applications, using our <u>Truths and/or Applications Resource</u>, from looking at Ruth's actions in chapter 2.

Day 3

- Naomi isn't mentioned much in this chapter, and this is one of the first things that stands out.

    - Do a quick summary of Naomi's sin in chapter 1. Do you see this same sin as an issue in chapter 2? Why do you think that Naomi isn't out gleaning in the fields? Are there any applications that you can make to your life from this example?

    - **How do you see Naomi respond to the Lord's kindness** through Boaz in verses 19-23? Let's look back over our lives. Has God's kindness ever softened our hearts? How? Let's take some time to process these questions in our journals.

Day 4

- » It's time to turn our eyes to Boaz.

  - o Before we make a list of what Boaz does in chapter 2, let's look at verse 1 and see how he is described. What characterizes Boaz?

  - o Let's use our Word Study Resource to look at **"a man of excellence."** (Other translations may say worthy, mighty, vallor, or man of great wealth.) Strongs #2428. What do you learn about the character of our story's hero?

  - o *Reaching further: Let's get a little more insight into who Boaz is. Look up this cross reference: 1 Chronicles 2:10-11. What is Boaz's heritage?*

  - o Now we are going to use our Listing Resource to note in our journals what Boaz says and does in chapter 2. What do you learn about Boaz and his character? How does he treat the people around him?

  - o Let's look a bit more at **the circumstances surrounding Boaz**. Review chapter 1:1 and 1:6. What insight do we see about Boaz and his choices? How do his actions differ from his relatives? What application can we draw about making a stand to follow God when you're family and friends chose not to?

- If we learn what a godly man looks like, we can better know what to look for, respect, and admire in the men of our lives. God calls Boaz 'A Man of Excellence.' Based on what you have observed in Boaz's life, what does a man of excellence look like? **Make a separate list titled "Man of Excellence" and jot down any qualities that stand out.** We will continue to add to this list throughout the rest of the study.

- Let's add to our list of Truths and Applications from looking at Boaz's actions.

Ruth: In the Shadow of His Wings

We have already seen Naomi in chapter 1 choose disobedience and reap bitterness. In chapter 2 we begin seeing a related concept brought out - **REWARD FOR OBEDIENCE**. Let's look and see how Ruth and Boaz demonstrate this.

- » How do we see Ruth reap a reward for obedience to God? What about Boaz?

- » **If this is true in the lives of Ruth and Boaz, how is this true in our lives?** Let's use our Cross References Resource to help flesh out and explain how God's kindness rewards us in our obedience. Perhaps start in Galatians 5:19-23 to see the fruit of obeying the Holy Spirit versus what comes from fleshly deeds.

Ruth, Boaz, and Naomi are each surrounded by their own circumstances. As you sum up what you learned about each character this week, include what you learned about how they deal with the situations around them.

Finally, what circumstances did you write down for yourself? Prayerfully evaluate how you are responding to your circumstance as you journal any takeaways from this lesson's study.

For such a short story, Ruth packs quite a lot into its tale. Let's rest and savor what we have learned. Next week, things are going to shake up.

Truths & Applications

Discipling Her

Suggestions for Leaders & Disciple-Makers

» This week, we focused on our three main characters and how they are choosing to respond to their circumstances. What are their circumstances?

» How does Ruth respond to her circumstances? What about Boaz? And what about Naomi?

» What does this reveal about their character? What does this say about where they are finding refuge?

» Think about your life. What are common "places of refuge" that you run to? Do these places help you obey God or disobey God?

» What does it mean practically for you to seek refuge in God?

» What did you learn about what makes a "man of excellence"? Do you know any men like this?

» Finally, how have you seen the rewards of obedience in your life?

week 4
CHAPTER 3: RISKY REDEMPTION

What comes to your mind when you think about redemption? Is it that "once lost and now found" type of identity? Is it a state of mind that is dependent on how we feel at the moment? Or is it just something we do when we pull up our Starbucks app and pray for some leftover money on a gift card?

Regardless of where we land on that spectrum, it does not negate the fact that the entire Bible is a story of redemption, including the story of Ruth. So far she has been married, widowed, and labeled a foreigner, taken a journey, and found a new career as a gleaner. **Now it's time for another step: her redemption. Let's see how it goes down.**

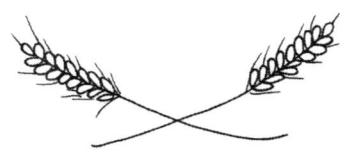

Day 1

Let's begin by prayerfully reading through Ruth 3 a few times. It will be helpful to read a few <u>translations</u>.

- » Now let's delve further into the Word together by marking all the references to our key players and add to our list for each character:
    - o Naomi
    - o Ruth
    - o Boaz

Day 2

Our story is beginning to get complicated. Let's look at a small section of verses at a time to see if we can figure it all out.

Reread Ruth 3:1-5 - Naomi and Ruth

- » Naomi immediately sets out a goal for Ruth. Write out the steps. What is Naomi's reasoning behind all of this? What is she hoping for?

- » Let's use our <u>Word Study Resource</u> from verse 1 for the Hebrew word "well" or "well provided for" (Strong's #3190). What do we learn? How does this show how Naomi views Ruth?

- » Now Naomi sets out a list of instructions for Ruth. Let's make a specific list of what she's telling Ruth to do by using our <u>Listing Resource</u>.

    - o These might not be the instructions we would give if we were Naomi, but there is definitely purpose in her tone. What do you think are Naomi's hopes in giving Ruth these specific instructions?

Ruth: In the Shadow of His Wings

» Are there any Truths and/or Applications for us from Naomi and Ruth's interactions? Let's begin a list for each by using our Truths and Applications Resources for a refresher.

Day 3 & 4

Reread Ruth 3:6-15 - Boaz and Ruth

Now the story is about to get interesting ... and strange (well, to us at least). **Let's move slowly through the text to absorb all that we can by using our** Summarizing Resource **to go verse by verse.**

- » As we look specifically at Ruth, what about her actions/words stand out? What do they say about her character? If you were in her position, would you do/say the same?

    - ○ **What about Ruth's obedience can we apply to our own lives** - especially when obedience takes us out of our comfort zone?

- » Now, let's look at this from the perspective of Boaz. What about his actions/words stand out? What do they say about his character?

- » **Specifically in verses 9-13 we see the concept of the "guardian-redeemer."** Other translations may say close relative/redeemer/kinsman /redeemer/etc. Let's take time to figure out this concept as it is important to the entire narrative. We'll begin by using our Word Study Resource for guardian/redeemer - Strong's #1350. Let's take note of what we learn in our journals from the definition.

- o Now, let's go to some Old Testament cross references to give some clarity. Do a quick read-through of Leviticus 25 and 27 and Deuteronomy 25 and answer the following questions: What were God's purposes for the guardian-redeemer? What do you learn about God's character and His provision for His people?

- o *Reaching Further: We can understand this concept better if we see other uses of the term guardian-redeemer throughout the rest of the Bible. The best way is to look at cross references where this same word was used. What do you learn about this term as it is used throughout the Bible?*

» Now that we have context, what do you think about what's just played out between Ruth and Boaz?

» Let's look specifically at verse 11. How does Boaz describe Ruth?

- o This term "woman of excellence" (worthy woman, woman of noble character) comes from the same word used to describe Boaz in chapter 2:1. We've seen that Boaz is a person to emulate by adding attributes of Boaz to our "man of excellence" list. Let's make a list for Ruth as well as she is also worthy of imitation. Go back through the first three chapters of Ruth and make a list of everything that sets her apart as a "woman of excellence."

- Why is Ruth a "woman of excellence"? Which of her character traits made the most impact on you?

» Like the sections before us, we want to keep at the forefront of our mind any Truths and/or Applications that will become our takeaways for the week. Let's make sure to add them to our growing list.

Day 5

Reread Ruth 3:16-18 - Naomi and Ruth

- » Now Ruth has to report back to her mother-in-law all that had gone down the night before. Explain their conversation in your own words.

- » What is Naomi's summation of Boaz? Go back to 3:1 and do a comparison. Let's take note of what we learn.

- » We've gotten to watch a progression in Naomi since we started reading this book. Is Naomi the same woman that showed up in Bethlehem in Chapter 1? Why or why not?

    - o Let's take time to prayerfully check our own mindsets. Are we stuck in the mire of focus on our sin and its consequences? Is our perspective based on truth or the circumstances we are experiencing?

- » Are there any other Truths and/or Applications for us from this section?

Ruth's redemption has just begun. Does her risk pay off? We won't know until we continue our study! In the meantime, go back through the story of Ruth 3 and make sure to write your summation for each main character. What main takeaways are being revealed to you? Prayerfully bring them to God, asking for His clarity and direction for your life this week.

Truths & Applications

Discipling Her

Suggestions for Leaders & Disciple-Makers

- » Let's begin with an overview of what happened in this chapter. What events took place?

- » What does Naomi tell Ruth to do? Why? What is Naomi's motivation?

- » Does Ruth obey? What does this tell you about her character?

- » What are you learning about becoming a "Woman of Excellence" from Ruth? What has stuck out to you the most?

- » What happens between Ruth and Boaz? What are their attitudes toward each other?

- » What is a "redeemer"? What did you learn by looking up the cross references?

- » Do you learn anything more about Boaz's character?

- » Do you see a change taking place in Naomi? What hints are we given that her heart is changing?

CHAPTER 4: GRAND FINALE

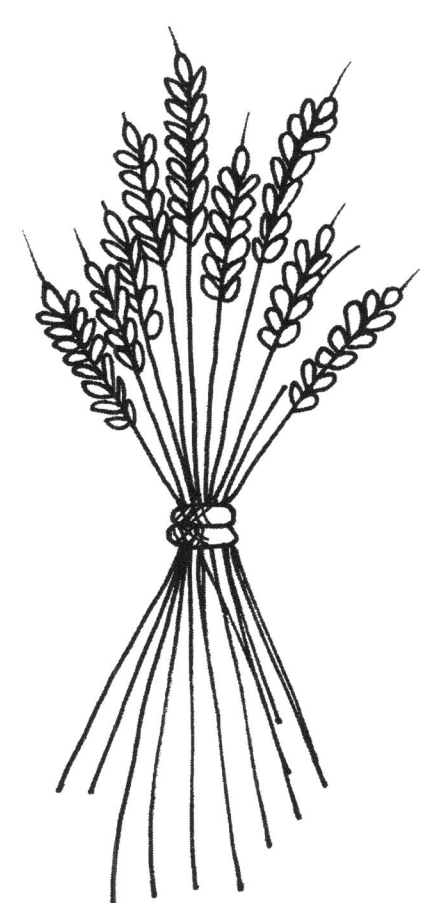

Ruth: In the Shadow of His Wings

It's time for the grand finale of our story! We left off with Ruth coming to Boaz to respectfully ask him to redeem her. The story is put into Boaz's hands. Let's jump in and see how Boaz proceeds while we glean some great truth from the redemption of Ruth and Naomi.

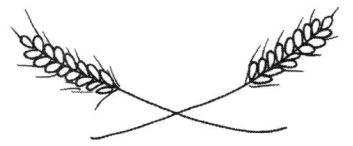

Day 1

- » Prayerfully read through Ruth 4 like you would a good book. Perhaps grab a cup of coffee or tea and watch what God does.

- » With a second reading we can use our <u>Key Word Resource</u> to mark our main characters. We'll also be adding another character this week - the "closer relative."

#

Reread Ruth 4:1-12 - Boaz versus the "Closer Relative"

» Let's use our <u>Summarizing Resource</u> for these verses to give ourselves a working knowledge of what Boaz is doing.

» There are two main men in this section: Boaz and the "closer relative" (also read as "guardian-redeemer" or just "redeemer" in verse 1). **Let's compare these two men** and see how they handle their God-given responsibilities. Make a short list of the actions you see each man taking. What do you learn?

» Review the work you did last week on the **guardian-redeemer** (perhaps even reread Deuteronomy 25:5-10). In light of the Law, how is the "closer relative" treated in this story? Can we draw any applications for how to treat people who don't do what they should?

» What other insight can we gain about the "closer relative" in this story? Are there things that we choose not to do because the costs seems too high?

» God is neither manipulating or controlling. He tells us what is best for us and we (like the "closer relative") can choose whether or not to obey. **Let's look a bit closer at how God desires us to handle our responsibilities.** Let's use our Cross Reference Resource to flesh out this concept. We can start in Matthew 25:14-30 or 2 Corinthians 9:7 and go from there.

» In this chapter, Boaz is presented with a tricky problem. He wants to redeem Ruth and Naomi, but there is a man in the way. How do you see him handle this problem? Look up Matthew 10:16 and any cross references in Proverbs to **meditate on how God calls us to be wise.**

» Before moving forward, let's think about Boaz and his actions. Add his attributes to our "man of excellence" list. **How would you summarize to someone else what a "man of excellence" looks like?**

» *Reaching Further: Look up the story of Tamar and Judah (Genesis 38). How is it similar to the story of Ruth? How does it differ?*

Day 3

Reread Ruth 4:9-17 - The Redeemed

Boaz obeyed God by acting out the part of the guardian-redeemer for Ruth and Naomi. **Let's look at the result of this redemption.** Start in verse 9 and re-read this passage, making note of all our key players (Naomi, Ruth, Boaz, and we're going to add Obed and the Lord).

- » Let's look closely at **Naomi** and use our Listing Resource to note what she says and does. Is she the same woman we met at the beginning of the book of Ruth? If no, what has changed? **What role did the lovingkindness of the Lord (Romans 2:4) play in the life of Naomi?** Are there any applications for us in this example?

- » Next, let's look at **Ruth** and list what we learn about her. How do the people of Bethlehem speak about her? What do you learn about her character? Add her attributes to our **"woman of excellence"** list. What about Ruth's life can we emulate?

- » In verse 13 we see something specific about Ruth. What does the Lord enable Ruth to do? What does this imply that she had not been able to do while married to Mahlon and living in Moab?

- o This is a painful topic for many people because it deals with not having something we want. Is there anything in your life that you want yet do not have? **Take some time and deal with any items that God has allowed to be given or kept from you. If this is a struggle, that's ok.** Keep working on it as we look at the character of the Lord at the end of this section.

» **Obed** is the next main character. Who is he? What will he do? Think on the idea of his role, and we will look more at the concept of redemption next week.

» Finally, what do you learn about **the Lord**? What is His role in this story? Moreover, who is given credit for the workings of the story of Ruth? What about our lives?

- o Let's read Romans 8:28. Does this give any further insight into God's hand in the story of Ruth or the story of our lives?

Day 4

Reread Ruth 4:16-22 The Lineage

> » Boaz and Ruth both obeyed God in faith. How do we see God blessing their actions? In your journal draw out the genealogy you see in verses 16-22. Next, let's look up Matthew 1:1-16 and continue the genealogy to see who else descends from Boaz and Ruth.

> » In light of what we just learned, what consequences does the "closer relative" have because he chose NOT to fulfill his responsibility found in the Law as guardian-redeemer? How can we apply this truth to our lives?

As women we can relate to both Ruth and Naomi. Before we finish, let's spend a few more minutes comparing these two women.

> » Naomi made some bad choices; and let's face it, we all do. The consequences of her choices were dire in her life. The consequences of sin are ALWAYS dire (Romans 3:23). **Review the book of Ruth and make note of Ruth's choices vs. Naomi's choices** (a short, generalized list will be easiest way to do this). Compare the two women's choices and the results of those

Ruth: In the Shadow of His Wings

choices. How do their choices affect one another? Can you draw any applications to your own life from Ruth and Naomi's example?

» How would you describe how Ruth and Naomi responded to their circumstance throughout the story? For comparison's sake, how would you describe The Lord's treatment of Ruth and Naomi? How do you believe the Lord treats you?

» *Reaching Further: Let's use our* Cross Reference Resource *to learn truth about how the Lord treats us. We can start in Jeremiah 29:11 and go from there.*

#

As we close this week, let's create some closure by summing up what we learned about each of our main characters, including the Lord. Using our Truths and/or Applications Resource what did God show us through the lives of Naomi, Ruth, and Boaz? What did the Lord show us about Himself? Are there any takeaways that we can carry with us?

Next week we will look back over the book of Ruth and really dig into the concept of redemption and resting in the refuge of His wings. It's an encore that will make the book of Ruth come alive.

Truths & Applications

Discipling Her

Suggestions for Leaders & Disciple-Makers

» What did you learn about Boaz and the "closer relative" in this chapter? How did they handle their responsibilities? Through watching Boaz, do you have a better picture of what a "man of excellence" acts like?

» Naomi and Ruth are finally redeemed. What affect does this have on Naomi and Ruth?

» What do the people in the town say about Ruth and Naomi?

» What do you learn about Obed?

» And finally what do you learn about God through this story? What is His character? Even when mistakes are made, how does God respond to the characters in this story -- and how does He respond to us?

week 6

A LOOK AT REDEMPTION

Ruth: In the Shadow of His Wings

Our time spent in the story of Ruth has been rich. It seems like within every verse there is a mirror where we can find identification with the narrative and application for our lives. But we don't want to walk away without focusing on the true theme of Ruth: *redemption*. This week let's take redemption out of the confines of Moab and Judah.

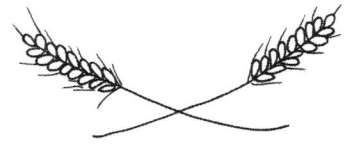

Day 1

Begin with a prayer that asks God to show Himself to us through the overarching story of Naomi, Ruth, and Boaz, and that He would teach us the importance and mind-blowing nature of redemption.

Let's take time to go back through the book of Ruth and take note of the following:

- Main Characters - What struck you about each individual? How did they evolve through the story?
  - Character of God - What major attributes of God were apparent in the story? Which changed or evolved your view of God?
  - Man and Woman of Excellence - What characteristics from our lists stood out to you? Which do you need to begin to practice?
- Major Truths - What big truths about God and/or yourself were apparent from our study?
  - Major Applications - What important applications, both internal and external, is God asking you to implement in your life right now?

Day 2

With Day 1's foundation of information in mind, let's tackle our theme: Redemption.

In Ruth's story, God used Boaz as her guardian-redeemer. When Boaz claims Ruth, not only is she redeemed, but Naomi and the family line of Elimelech are redeemed as well, all the way to King David and Jesus as we learned last week. **But what does the redemption of Ruth's family mean for us?**

- » Let's look at a New Testament perspective of redemption as a starting place. Read Galatians 4:1-7 and take note of what we learn about Jesus.

- » Now, using our <u>Word Study Resource</u>, let's review what we studied from Week 4 for the Hebrew for "guardian-redeemer" (Strong's #1350) and compare that to the Greek New Testament word for "redeem" we saw in the Galatians passage (Strong's #1805).

    - o What stands out to you about this definition? Who is the ultimate redeemer of mankind? How would you then explain Boaz's role as compared to Christ's?

    - o What does this mean for us?

#

The entirety of the Bible is a retelling of God's story. **And God's story is centered on His willingness to offer Jesus as our Redeemer.** So let's take some time to look at our Redeemer.

» Let's read through the following cross references. There are quite a few (and they are all quite good!), so feel free to do as many as you have time. Let's jot down in our journals what we learn from each.

- Mark 10:45
- John 3:16-17 and 10:14-15
- Romans 10:8-13
- Galatians 2:15-21 and 3:13-14
- Titus 2:11-14 and 3:4-7
- Hebrews 2 and 10:12
- 1 Peter 1:18-19

o **Our identity as followers of Christ hinges on the fact that we are redeemed, so understanding our Savior is extremely important.** Looking back over what we read, what did we learn about Jesus as our Redeemer? What do we learn about us as the redeemed?

- *Reaching Further: Find any other cross references through the New Testament (Acts - Revelation) that identify Jesus as our redeemer.*

- Can you identify any big overarching Truths and/or Applications?

Day 4

Like the preview of a coming attraction before the main event, Boaz was just a picture of the redemption that is available through Jesus. And what a picture God gave us, especially when we consider the context of the time period and culture of Israel! But is Boaz the only picture of redemption God gives us in the Old Testament? Can we see redemption throughout the entire Bible?

» Let's skim through God's Word remembering big stories and happenings and characters that God has revealed to us. See if you can see **redemption** either by the work of the Lord or His people. An example you could start with is the story of Joseph in Genesis. Let's make a list and take note of what stands out.

» We should be able to see a pattern of redemption throughout the entire narrative of the Bible. What does this say about God and His plan for humanity? For you? Have you considered the wonder of your own redemption?

Day 5

One last task before we are finished. **When looking at the role of the redeemer in the Old Testament, there were typically some criteria that would be met:**

- » There had to be a crisis.

- » There needed to be a relative.

- » The relative had to be wealthy or have high value.

- » The relative had to be willing.

- » Redemption was complete when the price was paid in full.

To summarize all we have learned, let's apply these criteria to two individuals.

- » First, let's identify and summarize Ruth's redeemer by applying all 5 to Boaz including specific references to Scripture that back up our claims.

- » Then, let's identify and summarize our Redeemer by applying the criteria to Jesus.

> » In your own words, how would you describe "redemption" to someone else? How would you summarize the book of Ruth and its theme/purpose?

Ruth's story has been rich! The lives of Naomi, Ruth, Boaz, and the unnamed closer relative converged during their separate journeys and provided so much wisdom. **Just like them, we are all at some point in our story. And no matter where we are in life, we can identify with one of the characters.** We may be a stranger to God. We may not know Him well, but we've said we're "all in." We may be on the cusp of redemption. We may be working from past redemption reaping the blessings of a life spent living for Christ. We may be leading others to redemption.

Wherever you are in the narrative, redemption is there. It's right within our reach.

"The LORD repay you for what you have done, and a full reward be given you by the LORD, the God of Israel, under whose wings you have come to take refuge!" Ruth 2:12

Truths & Applications

Discipling Her

Suggestions for Leaders & Disciple-Makers

» Look over your definitions of "redeemer" and "redeem" from both the Old and New Testaments. What did you learn?

» Why is your understanding of redemption so important in the study of Ruth and the entire Bible? Were you able to see Scripture in a new light?

» When you looked at the cross references in the New Testament, what did you learn about Jesus? Why is this important to your salvation?

» Do you recognize any of the same characteristics in Boaz and Jesus? Does watching Boaz help you understand Jesus?

» What other characters or events in Scripture help you understand redemption?

» Where have you most identified with Ruth's story? What is something you will carry with you as you end this study?

Made in the USA
San Bernardino, CA
27 April 2017